WYNNS

The First 100 Years

by

John Wynn

P. M. Heaton Publishing
Abergavenny, Gwent
Great Britain
1995

Front cover: John Fowler Steam Road Locomotive DW 2121 which has been privately preserved and Pacific Drawbar tractor GDW 585.

Title Page: Being hauled by two Pacific Drawbar tractors, a Column Box 69ft 1ins x 14ft x 14ft, weighing 72 tons, en route from Wrexham to the new plant of Air Products Ltd., at Ebbw Vale, where it was erected in a vertical position. Shown on the ascent of the notorious 1 in 6 Black Rock Hill.

Back Cover: The Author and driver Rex Evans standing in front of three Pacific tractors.
AND a very mixed bag of four tractors – Ward La France wrecker, Foden, Pacific and Scammell Pioneer working hard to ascend the steep access at the National Oil Refinery at Llandarcy.

ISBN 1 872006 09 4

© First Edition October, 1995
John Wynn and P. M. Heaton

Published by P. M. Heaton Publishing
Abergavenny, Gwent, NP7 9UH

Printed in Great Britain by
The Amadeus Press Ltd.,
Huddersfield, West Yorkshire, HD2 1YJ

Typesetting by Highlight Type Bureau Ltd.,
Bradford, West Yorkshire, BD8 7BY

Thomas Wynn
1821-1878

PREFACE

It is with considerable pleasure that I have selected the photographs and written the text and captions for this book. My great-grandfather, Thomas Wynn, founded the firm which was to evolve into Robert Wynn and Sons Ltd; more simply known to most as just WYNNS. For a firm which remained for a century under the directions and control of a single family – and which held a prominent place in the annals of road haulage, and particularly in heavy haulage, I feel with pride that much was achieved. This feeling is happily held by many others, not least by those who spent their working lives with the firm.

This is I hope the first of two books devoted to WYNNS, and in this volume I have taken the history in text and photographs up to 1963 when the centenary of the business was celebrated. In the later book I will deal with further developments, and particularly the International dimension.

To all those who have kindly helped in any way, with photographs, information or time – I thank you all.

John Wynn
Newport

October, 1995

Robert Wynn
1863-1923

WYNNS

The renowned haulage business, best remembered simply as WYNNS, was established at Newport, Monmouthshire in 1863. It was in that year that Thomas Wynn left his employment as foreman carriage cleaner at Newport High Street, and set himself up as a carrier – as haulage contractors were known in those days – with a couple of horses and carts.

Thomas who was born in 1821 hailed from Uffculme, near Cullumpton in Devon, and had commenced his working life as a contract carriage cleaner at Exeter St. Davids. Eventually he found his way to Paddington, and thereafter to Newport, where at some stage he became directly employed by the railway company.

He quickly identified the problem of transport in the Monmouthshire valleys. Goods, in ever increasing quantities, were coming down the main line to Newport, but there were only the canals or pack horses and mules for onward distribution. Thus he set himself up in business to take advantage of the opportunities which were presented. Apart from goods brought directly to Newport by rail, he formed an association with the Star Flour Mills in Newport and was soon distributing their flour to the bakeries and shops in the valleys. This connection continued right up until the mid 1950s, as the firm Thomas founded was still carrying their products until the mill was closed to make way for Kingsway. The connection with the railway was not severed either, as the firm acted as one of their agents at Newport, and undertook local deliveries from the High Street Goods yard for the best part of a century.

The founder of the business had ten children – two sons and eight daughters. Robert Wynn, from whom the business was to take its name, was only fifteen when his father died in 1878, by which time the firm had expanded to several dozen horses and carts. Robert with the aid of his elder sister, Emma, carried on the business. It is said that the young Robert was then too small to put the collars over the heads of the Shire horses, and his sister had to do this.

Four years later, and not yet twenty, Robert married Nora Small, the daughter of Samuel Small, a prominent haulier in Newport who specialised in the extraction of round timber from the surrounding forests. Two years later his father-in-law died, and although Robert was offered this business he insisted that it should go to auction, where he bought it. This was how WYNNS became involved with the extraction of timber, and during the Second World War, expanded into mid-Wales with a depot at Welshpool. This side of the business was discontinued in 1964 due to the then decline in the indiginous timber trade.

Robert and Nora Wynn
with their family

Family Scene, c.1900.
Sam Wynn holding the donkey's head, R.T. with the whip, a disgruntled George with nothing to hold, and the maid holding sister Hilda.

Expansion continued and Robert saw the possibilities for heavy haulage, with the rapid development of the steel works in Newport. In 1890, he had built in Newport a boiler wagon capable of hauling 40 tons which was used to carry heavy machinery from Mill Street railway sidings to the Lysaghts Steel Works in Corporation Road. Horses were still used as the form of propulsion and 48 were needed – four abreast – to pull the heaviest loads.

Robert and Nora Wynn also had ten children, but this time it was eight boys and two girls, of which two boys died in infancy. It was a reflection of the era that the eldest – Sam was twenty and had been involved in his father's business for some years when the youngest – Gordon was born in 1910. Of the six sons, five were to enter the firm. Transport must have also been in the girls' blood as one – Hilda, married Fred Sparkes, a haulier of some repute, who carried on his business from East Canal Wharf in Cardiff.

Steam power was introduced into the firm in the 1890s with the advent of steam traction engines and tractors. Nevertheless, horses still predominated, and even as late as the end of the 1920s over a hundred were being used. Robert entered farming primarily to produce the hay for the horses. For a time he had the Coldra Farm, on the hillside above what is now the Coldra Intersection of the M4 Motorway. He acquired 21 acres on Bettws Lane – which is now the playing fields of the High School – and rented land from the Corporation, including the Glebe Field off Caerleon Road.

Premises were acquired at 52, Shaftesbury Street, Newport, in 1902 – now the site of Sainsbury's supermarket – when Robert decided that the rapid expansion of the firm necessitated his 'living over the shop' as it were. In addition to a large yard there was also stabling for 200 horses, and several houses, two of which were occupied by Robert, Nora and their growing family. This subsequently became the headquarters office of the firm. After work on a Saturday all the horses were turned out until early on the Monday morning for grazing in his fields. No easy task to drive (herd) all these horses back and forth along the town's roads.

As soon as they were old enough Robert's three eldest sons – Sam (born 1890), Robert Thomas (known as R.T., and born in 1892) and George (born 1894) joined their father in the business. Much of the success of WYNNS could be attributed to the fact that there were subsequently five brothers in the firm, all actively participating in the business. Over the years, whilst eventually specialising in one department or another, in those years when the firm was rapidly expanding the brothers could be seen more than pulling their weight. All had spent years driving to all parts of the country, making sure that the job got done – as quickly as possible, and thus as profitably as possible.

With the First World War came the responsibility for moving much heavy war equipment mainly for the War Department, including heavy guns, and some of the firm's traction engines were commandeered for use by the Forces. However much of the equipment – and employees – were exempt, due to the firm's position in the war effort, including extraction of timber from the forests.

Early in 1923 Robert Wynn incorporated the business, as Robert Wynn and Sons Ltd., he holding 50% and his wife the other 50%. Alas in November, 1923 he died, leaving his share divided between the three eldest sons who had not as yet been joined in the firm by two of their younger brothers. It speaks highly of the brothers that when they sold the company in 1964, each of the five brothers involved and their families had an equal share. A true family venture.

In the early 1920s most of the traction engines were phased out. Percy Wynn, the next brother to enter the business, had been apprenticed to Fowlers of Leeds, and he had worked on the last engine during its building, this was to be DW2121.

These were replaced by Foden and subsequently Sentinel steam wagons, and it was with such vehicles that R.T. and Percy Wynn commenced what came to be known as the 'London trunk' – carrying tin plate from the Mellingriffith works at Whitchurch, returning with Cross & Blackwells products, bacon, Chinese eggs, and Sharps toffees for delivery to Pan Produce in Dock Street, and other wholesalers in and around Newport.

Through their association with Mabley Parker, the public works contractor at Taffs Wells, the company expanded into Cardiff. A yard and stables were rented in Cairn Street, now Rhymney Terrace, in Cathays, and a few rooms for office and storage in Zammits Building on the corner of Herbert Street and Bute Street. This part of the business was supervised by R.T. who subsequently moved to Cardiff to live.

The days of steam were now numbered. The Road Traffic Act, 1930, introduced a gross weight limit of 24 tons. The motive unit itself, all up with coal and water, weighed 13 tons, plus the trailer another 3 tons, just leaving a payload of 8 tons, against the previous 25. This was just not profitable. Thus the Foden and Sentinel steam wagons were phased out as regards the London trunk, but some were kept for use on the East Dock for tar spraying contracts in and around the City. Steam from the boiler being pumped to the tank to keep the tar warm and in liquid form.

On the London trunk, steam was replaced by six and eight wheel Scammells. In 1930 the youngest of the five brothers, Gordon Wynn, went to the London depot to manage operations. Substantial tonnages were then moved between South Wales and London in both directions each night. By the time of nationalisation in 1947, some forty vehicles were employed on this route.

The business in Cardiff grew. The company was engaged – also by Mabley Parker – to provide the horses and tip carts in the building of Western Avenue and this led to a contract with Cardiff Corporation. That contract – first to provide horses and tip carts, subsequently replaced by Bedford tippers – lasted until 1966, when WYNNS decided to pull out of tippers.

The Wynn Family celebrate the end of the Second World War in 1945 – Third Generation in Second Row (from left) Gordon (G.P.), Alan (who did not enter the business, but was a farmer), Hilda, George (O.G.), Sam, Robert Thomas (R.T.), Percy (H.P.) and Emma. O.G.'s son John is 4th from left in front row, R.T.'s son Noel is 4th from right back row, and Sam's son Bob is extreme right back row.

Vast quantities of heavy equipment was moved during the Second World War, and the company helped the war effort in whatever way required.

Immediately post-war, the demand for even heavier capacity, entailed the construction of the first 120 ton trailer, largely in WYNNS own workshops. This was quickly used to transport the hammer blocks of 110 tons for the works of Northern Aluminium at Rogerstone. The Steel Company of Wales developed Margam works and this brought much heavy haulage work to the company. The demand for electricity increased, bringing with it the need for building power stations and electricity substations, and thus there was great demand for heavy haulage.

With the nationalisation of the coal industry, the big customer Powell Duffryn's pits were taken over by the National Coal Board. However, Powell Duffryn's fleet of tankers which also passed into the N.C.B.'s control, were not acquired with any enthusiasm. The Coal Board preferred to contract transport, so that WYNNS bought these steamers and carried out the haulage for them. This contract which lasted until 1981, was to have an important part in the firm's fortunes under the nationalisation of road transport under the Attlee Government.

The 1947 Road Transport Act provided for the compulsory acquisition by the British Transport Commission of haulage businesses, but exempted those who could show that over half of their revenue came from what was termed 'exempted traffic' – namely: meat haulage, furniture removals, heavy haulage, bulk liquids and round timber. Thus with the ex-Powell Duffryn steamers, WYNNS escaped the net. They did however, lose their nightly trunk business to London, at this time. It was a considerable time before we were paid.

Many of WYNNS competitors were nationalised, and were to disappear into the Pickfords concern. This left WYNNS as the only competitor to Pickfords, and not surprisingly many old and new customers were anxious for the company not to disappear. Considerable support was forthcoming for WYNNS as a result.

Whilst Pickfords had a contract with the North British Locomotive Company to transport locomotives from their works at Glasgow to the docks, for shipment to India, Percy Wynn heard about the intention for one of these to be displayed at the Festival of Britain exhibition in London. It was to be shipped from Glasgow to London by sea, where it was to be hauled to the exhibition site and installed on a 3ft. 6in. plinth. Percy went straight to Glasgow where he persuaded the manufacturers that WYNNS should be awarded the contract in London. He succeeded, and quickly ordered the girders to go with the job. Much publicity was achieved by the company, and proved to be an important milestone.

Throughout the history of WYNNS, innovation had always been the name of the game. Just as Robert Wynn had seen the need for the 40 ton boiler wagon in 1890, his son Percy, who had an engineering bent, saw that WYNNS would secure a considerable advantage over Pickfords if they could get on to pneumatic tyres, which had been developed for earthmoving equipment; coupled with hydraulic suspension similar to that used in aircraft. Quietly, he approached Cranes of Dereham and Dunlops with his ideas which resulted in a 16 wheeled trailer capable of carrying 150 tons being delivered. This had been constructed entirely at the risk of WYNNS, neither Cranes or Dunlop being prepared to offer any guarantee. Pickfords were also impressed, as they quickly ordered a similar outfit. WYNNS soon trumped them, however, by ordering a bigger and better trailer.

It was not long before WYNNS came under pressure from the heavy electrical manufacturers – English Electric at Stafford, Metro Vickers at Trafford Park, Manchester, Parsons of Newcastle and others to expand into the North of England, so as to more effectively compete with Pickfords. This also coincided with denationalisation of road transport, and the opportunity was taken of acquiring from the Disposal Board fifteen tractors and trailers formerly belonging to Pickfords. Not that WYNNS wanted the vehicles, but more importantly the carriers' licences which came with them.

At this time Eddie Clark from Pickfords was recruited. He had been their deputy manager at their Manchester depot and brought with him a wealth of experience. As a result a depot was opened at Moss Side, Manchester.

After the war it had been difficult to obtain suitable heavy motive units. WYNNS had been impressed with what they saw of the U.S. Army vehicles seen in the United Kingdom in the war years, and were quick to purchase six Pacific and up to thirty Diamond 'T' units. The Pacifics were petrol-engined, with a high fuel consumption, and were rapidly converted to diesel. These vehicles proved to be a most important acquisition in the history of the company. Many of them saw service into the 1970s and were constantly rebuilt and updated in WYNNS own workshops.

In 1963 WYNNS celebrated their centenary with a grand dinner in The Kings Head Hotel at Newport, and on the following Sunday the company took over the streets of Newport with a parade of their vehicles – a horse and cart leading, followed by the Fowler traction engine DW2121 towing the 73-year-old boiler wagon, and the rear brought up by their latest acquisition, a 48 wheeled 300 ton capacity trailer towed by a 450hp Scammell tractor.

Thus the business of Robert Wynn and Sons Ltd. celebrated its 100th birthday with a justifiable feeling of pride in its achievement as a leader in the haulage industry.

Whatever you have to move we will find a vehicle to move it.

"Robert Wynn & Sons Ltd."

Above left: A team of horses drawing a trailer laden with a tank locomotive c.1890. Horses were the main form of propulsion in the WYNNS fleet right up until the First World War, although their use was continued until 1939.

Below left: View showing some of the 200 horses employed by WYNNS c.1895.

Above: WYNNS use of horse drawn vehicles continued until the Second World War – When they were replaced by tipping lorries.

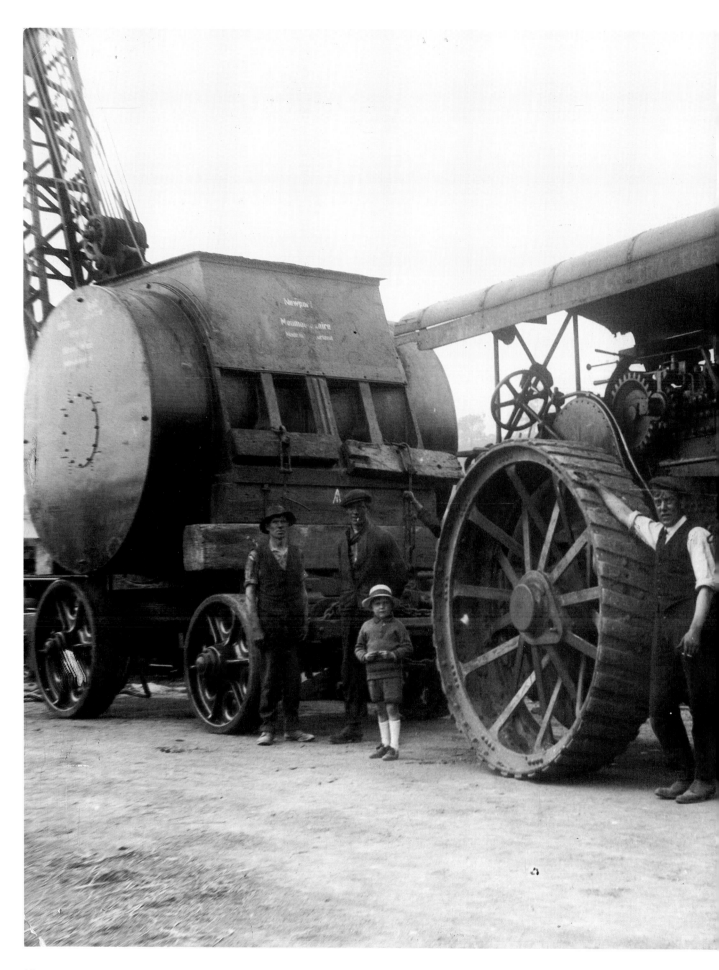

Steam power was introduced into the fleet of Robert Wynn and Sons in the 1890s. This photograph shows a 30 ton Stator for Newport Power Station in transit at Lliswerry Sidings in the 1920s. The drawing vehicle is a Fowler Road Locomotive DW 2121 bought new by the firm in July, 1920. H.P. (Percy) Wynn had worked on its construction at John Fowlers in Leeds where he had served his apprenticeship. Shown on the right is R.T. Wynn with his son Noel.

A Steam Traction Engine drawing a heavy gun barrel during the First World War. The rear wheels of the trailer have been extended to accommodate the length of the load.

A further view of DW 2121 at Lliswerry Sidings. Note that the rear wheels of the trailer have been closed up to carry the Stator. This vehicle was capable of carrying 40 tons, and had been built in the firm's own workshop.

A 26 ton Marine Boiler en route from Southampton to Cardiff in 1923. The leading engine is a Garrett Steam Road Locomotive DW 2119 (Chassis No. 33548) double-heading the Fowler DW 2121. DW 2119 was built in 1915 for A. Thomas of Caerleon, from whom Wynns bought her in March, 1921 when she was first registered. Although bought new in 1920 DW 2121 was first registered the following year.

DW 2119 leading and DW 2121 shown hauling three narrow gauge contractors locomotives from Newport to Llanvihangel Crucorney during the building of the Black Mountains Reservoir for the Abertillery and District Water Board.

Above: One of the main hazards to be overcome when delivering a load in the early days was the poor condition of the roads. This point is well illustrated in this view taken during the delivery of a 25 ton Electric Excavator to the Penarth Cement Company. The Traction Engine is again the Fowler DW 2121.

Left: DW 2121 was eventually relegated from the Heavy Haulage Fleet to Timber Extraction – as shown here.

WYNNS acquired their first petrol-engined lorry in June, 1916 – this being a Palladium 25hp, DW 999. This photograph shows three early motor lorries – from the left: Albion DW 526 with reissued registration and grey livery bought new in June, 1921, another grey coloured Albion DW 2844 new to the fleet in July, 1922, and DW 4 a Karrier 50hp bought new in June, 1919 but with re-issued registration mark. This was their second motor lorry. Note the carts on the right.

Another view of Albion motor lorry, DW 2844 which had an unladen weight of 2 tons 7cwt 2qrs.

This Foden steamer DW 4040 acquired in March, 1925 was WYNNS first articulated lorry, and is shown:–

Top left: Carrying a Marine boiler on solid-tyred low loader trailer in the 1920s.

Above: Hauling a cast iron wheel, 12ft 9ins in diameter from Cardiff to London in March, 1929.

Bottom left: Hauling a ship's propeller on a flat-bed trailer, driven by H.P. Wynn. Note the bags of coal fuel at the rear of the trailer.

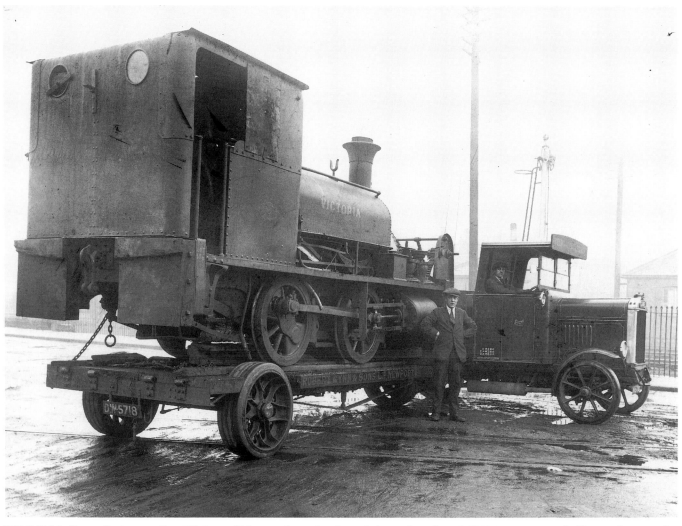

WYNNS first Scammell. This solid-tyred articulated low loader DW 5718 was delivered new in October, 1927. Shown carrying a locomotive in 1920, H.P. Wynn is in the driving seat and R.T. Wynn is stood alongside.

Whilst operating to all parts of the country, in the inter-war years a direct nightly trunk service was established between South Wales and London. Initially operated by Foden and Sentinel steam lorries, these were subsequently replaced by petrol and later diesel engined vehicles. At this time WYNNS had depots at Newport, Cardiff and London. Illustrated is a Sentinel articulated steamer DW 6440 (Fleet No. 25) bought new in March, 1929.

This pair of Scammell 'Super Six' lorries – DW 7652 (52) and DW 7653 (53) entered the WYNNS fleet in December, 1931, for service on the nightly trunk. DW 7653 was exhibited on the Scammell stand at the Earl's Court Commercial Motor Show in 1931.

An impressive view of the pair is shown overleaf.

NIGHTLY TRUNK SERVICE
LONDON ROBERT WYNN & SONS LTD.
NEWPORT - CARDIFF - LONDON.
SCAMMELL
53
DW 7653

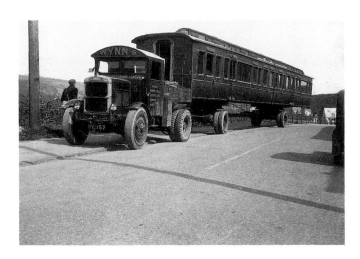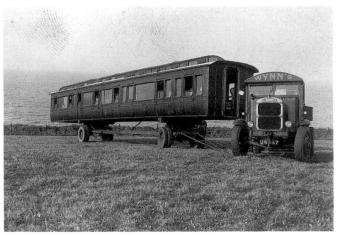

Shown on and off the road, this Scammell UW167 (12) is shown hauling a Royal coach as used by Queen Victoria, from Newcastle Emlyn Station to Aberporth on a trailer normally used for timber extraction. UW167 was new to W.E. Clarke, London in October, 1930, and was acquired in 1933 by WYNNS when they bought the Pearce Haulage Company fleet. The vehicle was rebuilt as a Timber Tractor, as shown, to a design of H.P. Wynn.

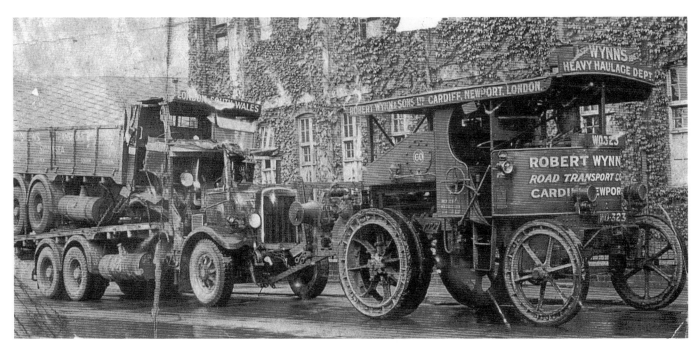

Sentinel Steam Timber Tractor WO323 (60) towing two damaged lorries owned by Entress Transport of Swansea. The vehicle was new in May, 1927 to Williams Bros., of 3, Ivor Houses, Pandy, and was rebuilt after crashing at a bridge near Brecon. She was bought by WYNNS in 1933.

Opposite: New to G. Earle, Hull in November, 1929 – KH9895 was a 45 ton articulated tractor unit which ran on solid tyres. Acquired by WYNNS in 1933 she is seen hauling a large diameter column.

Scammell 51 was an important unit in the Heavy Haulage fleet, as seen in these views carrying a variety of loads. She was eventually sold to Whayman of Pontypridd and not broken up until 1963.

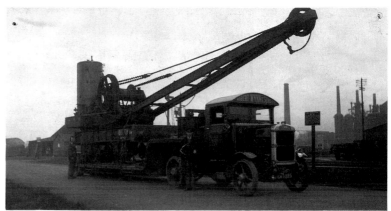

Owing to Security Regulations very few photographs of WYNNS war-time activities were allowed to be taken. This view of a Landing Craft moving through London was published in the London 'Evening News' on 3rd July, 1943, with the object of deceiving the enemy. KH9895 (51) certainly looked the part, and displayed an unusual amount of luck.

WYNNS

On the outside of this group are two Sentinel 'S' type 4 wheel steam lorries, as used with drawbar trailers on the nightly trunk service. – DW 8588 (76) and DW 8587 (75). In the centre are four Garner 6 wheel motor lorries DW 8631-4 (77-80).

Acquired during the Spring of 1934 they were used for local deliveries in South Wales having had their loads transhipped from the London Trunk.

Another view of the Sentinel steam lorries DW 8588 and DW 8587.

An example of the poor roads encountered. This Scammell rigid 6 wheel flat lorry (Fleet No. 71) loaded with a tracked vehicle is headed by Scammell Timber Tractor DW 9735 (35) in the 1930s. This latter vehicle was acquired in December, 1935.

Scammell Timber Tractor DW 9852 (49) was bought by WYNNS in February, 1936. She is seen about to set out with a heavy load for delivery to a Sawmill.

The extraction of round timber. WYNNS had been involved in this business since 1885, and continued with it for 80 years. This view shows the heavy trunks with trailer alongside prior to loading.

The Scammell Timber Tractor winching the trunks onto the trailer.

The trailer with its load is winched up a bank towards firmer ground, and eventually the road.

Scammell Timber Tractor ADW 616 (16) entered WYNNS fleet in February, 1937. When, in the blizzards of 1947, H.P. Wynn heard that four of the London-South Wales trunk lorries were stuck in the Cotswolds, he sent ADW 616 and crew to get them out. He quickly followed himself early the next day with Harry Thomas, and the vehicles were soon back in service. This photograph holds testimony to that fact.

Scammell 8 wheel rigid lorry ADW 617 (81) operating with a Dolly. Acquired in February, 1937 she was WYNNS first eight-wheeler. Eventually she was converted into a tar tanker.

Above: An exhibit for the Bristol Aeroplane Company en route to the Paris Air Show in 1938. The load is carried on a petrol-engined Bedford low loader – DW 9726 (27) first registered in January, 1936.

Opposite top: Scammell 45 ton 4 x 2 chain drive motive unit for hauling heavy duty low loaders. Units of this type were powered by Gardner 6 cylinder 102bhp diesel engines, and equipped with four speed gearboxes. This example shown new was purchased by WYNNS in November, 1938 and was fitted with solid tyres at the rear. Numbered CDW 33 she carried Fleet No. 87.

Opposite bottom: Another view of the Scammell tractor CDW 33 (87) shown hauling a large gun barrell during the Second World War. Now fitted with pneumatic tyres on the rear axle. This vehicle was the first of a batch of this type owned by WYNNS – and was an important asset in the Heavy Haulage Fleet.

Acquired by WYNNS in April, 1939 this Scammell 6 wheel rigid flat lorry, BLN963 (94) dating from January, 1935, was one of five which came from Fisher Renwick. The others being BLO690 (92), BXV560 (93), BLL835 (95) and BLL248(96). They became the backbone of the London Trunk Service, and passed to British Road Services between 1949-1951.

Although not easy to acquire new vehicles during the Second World War; due to the essential nature of their work WYNNS were allowed to buy some. Illustrated is a modern articulated outfit CDW 917 (103) which was one of three bought from ERF at Sandbach in 1941. The others being CDW 909 (101) and CDW 910 (102).

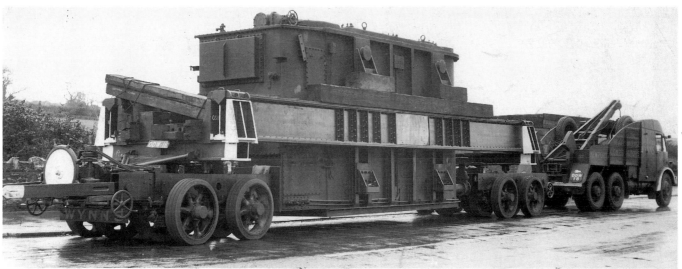

This Foden 6 wheel Drawbar Tractor DDW 18 (112) bought in February, 1942 was the mainstay of the WYNNS Heavy Haulage Fleet during the war years. Seen hauling a Landing Barge (top) and centre and bottom transporting a 30,000 KVA Transformer weighing 90 tons en route to a power station in October, 1943. The transformer is carried in slung position to clear overhead bridges. This Foden was one of only three of this type ever built.

Above: An impressive view of the Foden Drawbar tractor 112 hauling a solid-tyred trailer with a 100 ton Excavator. Assistance at the rear is provided by the Scammell 87 now temporarily ballasted.

Right: This Scotch Marine boiler was recovered off a beach at Pembroke and hauled to the Eastern Dry Dock, Newport. In the background can be seen the Corporation Road works of Messrs Stewart and Lloyd.

DDW 18(112) with laden solid-tyred trailer with CDW 33 (87) having just arrived at Cardiff Docks.

An English Electric Transformer with Foden No. 112 and solid-tyred low loader trailer. Note the absence of mudguards.

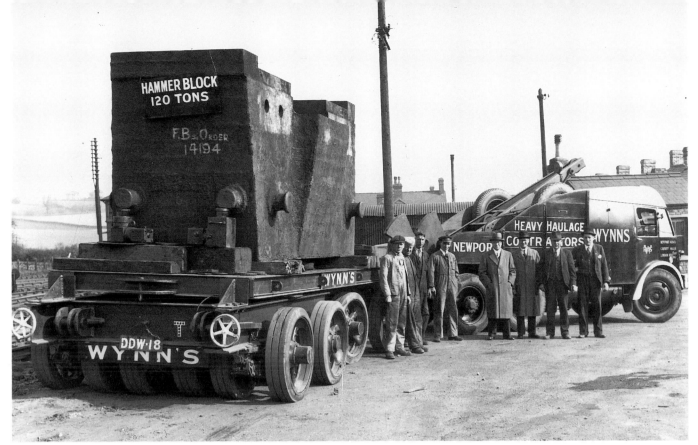

Above: DDW 18 ready to set out with this 120 ton Hammer Block for a site in Birmingham. Shown from the left: Jack Bleuitt, Alan Brown, Ern Adams, Bill Hayward, two customers, R.T. Wynn and H.P. Wynn and (*below*) Completing a difficult manoeuvre in the centre of Birmingham. The Foden is taken off the front of this long vessel and connected to the rear bogie whilst the local Fire Service assist on the front bogie. This problem was caused by the Police escort inadvertently taking the wrong route. The driver, Stan Phillips, not surprisingly, has never forgotten this incident.

Scammell Articulated lorry DDW 226 (132) which entered the WYNNS fleet in February, 1946, loaded with a motorised earth grader. The trailer was originally a U.S. Army 40ft cargo carrier.

Acquired in April, 1946 this Bedford OWLD 5 ton sided lorry DDW 287 (134) was normally used for local deliveries.

Looking from Shaftsbury Street, Newport at the entrance to the Headquarters and Yard of Robert Wynn and Sons Ltd., in the 1950s.

Looking from the yard at the Shaftsbury Street Depot towards the Main Road.

Five units of the Pearce Haulage Company fleet which had been owned by WYNNS since the early 1930s. On the left are two of the eight Foden GS 6 wheel flat lorries acquired as war surplus. These two were in the Pearce black livery – FDW 61 (66) and FDW 60 (65). Next is a pair of Scammell 6 wheel rigid flat lorries – BLO 690 (92) and BXV 560 (93) and the fifth vehicle is a Bedford OXC articulated unit DDW 30 which had arrived in the fleet in December, 1942.

With the post-war Nationalisation of the Road Transport Industry the Pearce fleet passed into the ownership of British Road Services in April, 1949. Whilst other vehicles were lost to nationalisation, the WYNNS fleet survived in the hands of the family, due to the majority of the business being involved in Heavy Haulage, Tankers, and Timber Extraction. However, by 1951 all the South Wales – London trunk lorries had passed into BRS ownership.

H.P. Wynn was driving along the Cardiff to Newport Road during the Second World War when he caught up with a convoy of American Diamond T tank transporters. The last vehicle had to brake suddenly causing a cloud of black smoke. He was so impressed by the braking capabilities of these outfits that he went back to the Shaftsbury Street yard where he picked up both George Wynn and the Author and took them back to show them the black tyre marks left on the road surface. No haulage company in Britain had ever had vehicles with such braking capabilities, and he looked forward to the day when WYNNS would have some of these in its Heavy Haulage Fleet. And so they did. Thirty Diamond T Drawbar tractors were eventually bought – and became the mainstay of the WYNNS fleet for around 25 years.

This photograph shows the two earliest Diamond Ts with a solid-tyred trailer in October, 1949. The load – an Ingot Buggy, measured 27ft 2ins long, 11ft 7ins wide, 12ft high, and weighed 100 tons, and was in transit from Newport Docks to the Steel Company of Wales, Abbey works, Margam.

The two Diamond T 980 tractors, had been purchased by WYNNS in May, 1947 – EDW 95 (160) and EDW 96 (161).

Diamond T, EDW 95 (160) is shown hard at work.

Opposite top: Coupled to a 16 wheel trailer loaded with a 100 ton transformer – inching forward in a tight space.

Opposite bottom: With part of an excavator for Sir Robert McAlpine. Loaded on two Dyson bolster trailers before the advent of rear stearing.

Above: Driver Arthur Matthews in the cab with Tom White and Ron Bailey standing at the front of the tractor, as it enters Fulham Power Station with the 80 ton outer casing of an electrical stator.

Above: This vessel was hauled to the B.P. Oil Refinery at Llandarcy from London in November, 1952 by Diamond T EDW 96 (161) again on the hard worked Dyson Trailers.

Left: This trailer headed by the same Diamond T Drawbar tractor is actually carrying the load it was designed to carry – a tank.

Above: A generator manufactured by the English Electric Co. Ltd., Stafford arriving at Stourport Power Station. Carried on a 16 wheel solid tyred trailer No. 302 and drawn by an early WYNNS Diamond T, the pushing vehicle being the 1938 Scammell CDW 33 (87) now fitted with a ballast box.

Below: This 75ft long, 130 ton Cracking Tower was delivered to the Llandarcy Oil Refinery in 1952 on two 16 wheel solid tyred bogies and towed by a Diamond T with a Scammell pushing. Bill Hayward was the driver of the leading vehicle.

In the immediate post-war period WYNNS bought ten of these army surplus FWD SU-COE Timber Tractors.

Entering service in May, 1950 this FWD SU-COE Timber Tractor FDW 79 (79) was resplendent in her newly applied paintwork, pictured in Shaftsbury Street.

With a Depot at Welshpool in Mid-Wales WYNNS had rapidly updated its fleet involved in Timber Extraction. In addition to the ten FWDs, by 1950 three new Unipower Forrester Timber tractors had entered service. In this view Unipower tractor FDW 912 (191) with timber laden trailer leads an FWD outfit FDW 77 (77) towards the main road.

WYNNS

Above: Two 93 ton Castings (Mill Housings) leaving the works of Davy-United at Sheffield in 1951 en route to the Steel Company of Wales, Abbey Works, Margam. The first is towed by a Diamond T, 981 Drawbar Tractor FDW 922 (186), which had entered service with WYNNS in April, 1950, with a Scammell pushing. The second outfit has a Diamond T at both ends. The leading vehicle was driven by Bryn Groves.

Opposite top: An impressive view of Diamond T EDW 868 double heading this 100 ton plus transformer near Andover. A Scammell 4 wheel Drawbar tractor brings up the rear.

Opposite bottom: FDW 533 which arrived in the fleet in June, 1949, pulls a 16 wheel solid tyred trailer with a vessel for the National Oil Refinery at Llandarcy.

Above: WYNNS operated a large fleet of mobile cranes – not only were they prepared to move anything, they were also prepared to recover or lift anything. A point well illustrated in this view of a Thornycroft-Coles crane lorry FDW 752 (207) assisting in the recovery of an AEC 8 wheel lorry, which was owned by Newport Haulier Terrence A. Johnsey, which had gone over an embankment near Usk.

Opposite: The Marquis of Bute being lifted into position in Cardiff's City Centre.

Whilst H.P. (Percy) Wynn was well satisfied with the performance of the Diamond T Drawbar tractors purchased, and fully intended buying more, he felt the need for an even heavier tractor. He was aware that the U.S. Army had been using Pacific M26 Drawbar tractors, and when he learnt of the location of around two dozen of these exceptional vehicles, for sale, lying in a quarry in Kent, he went and bought four at the bargain price of £400 each. In the event a total of six were purchased for use and another four for parts.

In their purchased condition (as illustrated) they were fitted with Hall Scott petrol engines of 177hp and Fuller crash gear boxes. They were driven by a chain drive to the rear axles. They had six forward and two reverse gears and a splitter drop box which gave a high and low ratio range. With their large petrol engines the Pacifics had a very high fuel consumption and when rebuilt were converted initially to Hercules (Diamond T) diesels, and subsequently to turbo-charged Cummins diesel engines. The turbo-charger was of the Roots type. This combination gave a horsepower of 180 and much improved fuel consumption. The gearboxes were also changed to the semi-automatic type which gave a smoother change and put less shock loading on the transmissions and engines.

These together with the Diamond T units were to remain the backbone of the WYNNS heavy Haulage fleet for some twenty years.

Whilst six had been bought for use, they were not all put into service immediately. In fact the rebuilding took place to suit the firm, and was done as and when they were needed – which in the event was between 1950 and 1964 as follows:–

Date into Fleet		Fleet No.	Registration	Name
September,	1950	192	GDW 277	Dreadnought
May,	1951	196	GDW 585	Helpmate
December,	1951	193	HDW 122	Conqueror
	1961	195	YDW 356	Challenger
	1962	194	1570DW	Valiant
December,	1964	197	ADW 228B	Enterprise

The rebuilt vehicles bore very little resemblance to when purchased as can be seen from the before and after photographs of GDW 277. Each vehicle bore its own individual name which had been chosen by the Author.

R.T. Wynn to brother H.P. "Are you sure it'll fit?". It provoked an appropriate response.

But happily it did.

This 105 ton locomotive was an exhibit at the Festival of Britain at London in 1951. Manufactured by the North British Locomotive Works in Glasgow it had been brought around from Glasgow to London by sea, where it was loaded onto WYNNS trailer No.302 at the Surrey Commercial Docks on 24th January, 1951 and conveyed through the streets of London to the Exhibition site at Battersea. Note the solid tyred wheels on the trailer. On the following page the locomotive and trailer is shown en route to its destination in charge of the first Pacific to enter service – GDW 277 (192) with a Scammell at the rear. The locomotive's tender was also moved (not shown) headed by a WYNNS Diamond T. Much publicity was obtained by WYNNS and it proved to be a milestone in the history of the firm. It must be remembered that with the nationalisation of the Road Transport Industry WYNNS were the only haulier apart from the state-owned Pickfords who could have moved this load. The words 'Free Enterprise' were appropriately displayed on the trailer. The girders for this trailer had only been delivered from the Fairfield yard at Chepstow the previous week, a point not lost on the representatives of Pickfords who watched the move – stunned. At the end of the exhibition the locomotive was transported by the firm back to the docks where it continued its journey to India. Again Pacific GDW 277 was used, but this time loaded on the first Crane 150 ton hydraulic suspension trailer with pneumatic tyres.

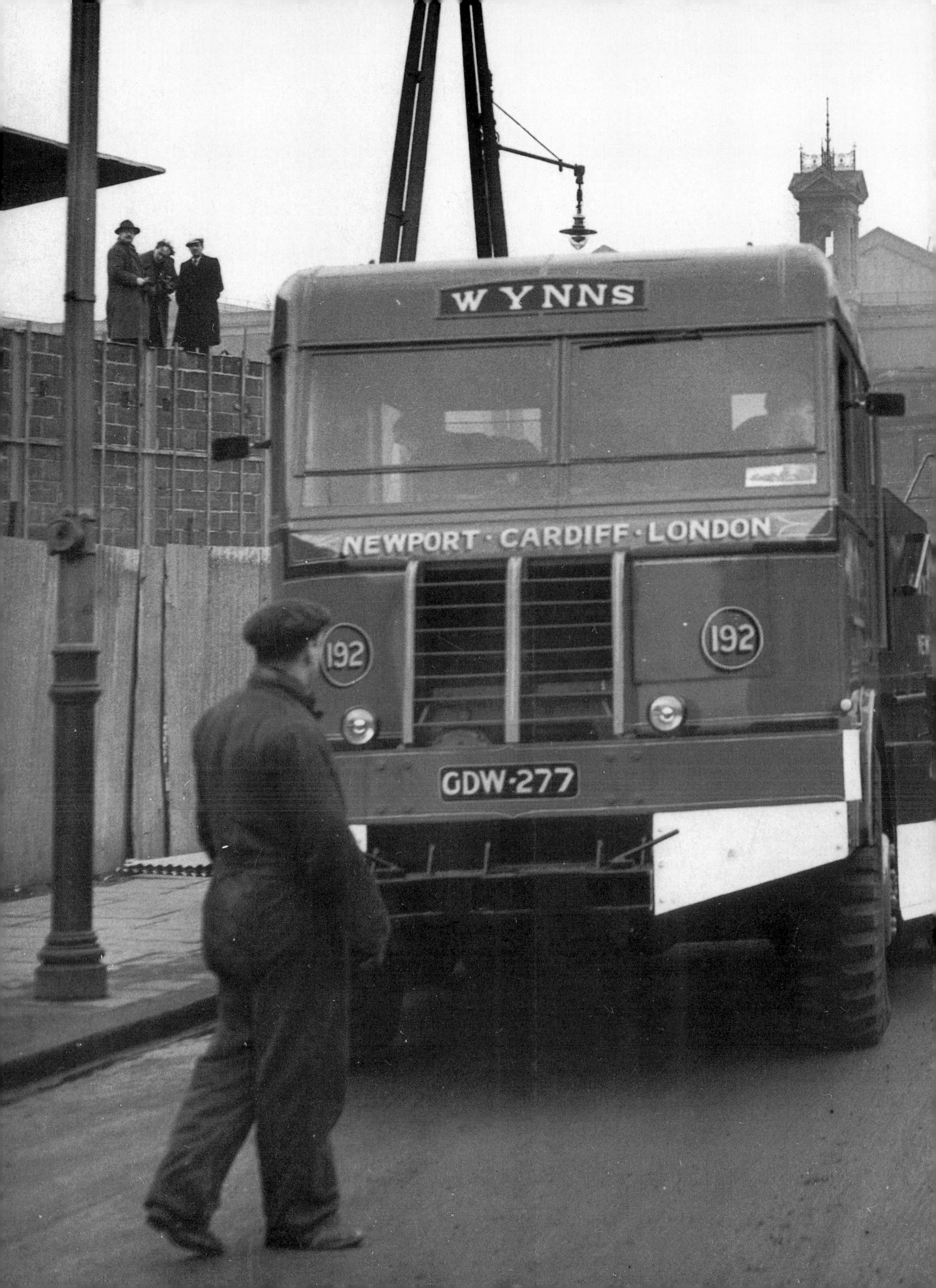
WYNNS
NEWPORT · CARDIFF · LONDON
192
192
GDW-277

Above: On arrival at the exhibition site Pacific GDW 277 and a Diamond T manoeuvre the locomotive into position for unloading. WYNNS Heavy Gang had to mount the locomotive on a 3ft 6ins high plinth.

WYNNS first Pacific hard at work.

Top: An impressive view of a Blackwood Hodge excavator leaving the manufacturer's works at Northampton. GDW 277 driven by Arthur Matthews, with a ballasted Scammell HDW 43 (210) driven by Archie Morgan pushing.

Above: The same combination of tractors, but with trailer 333s bogies fitted with a top girder set instead of the Swan neck frame. Shown carrying a 120 ton Ferranti transformer from Oldham to a Grid site at Slough, Berkshire, about to negotiate 'The Swan' island at Yardley, Birmingham in October, 1952.

Right: The largest and heaviest single piece of electrical equipment ever moved by road or rail in Great Britain up to that time. En route from BTH, Rugby to Staythorpe Grid Site. At 150 tons special dispensation was received from the trailer manufacturer – Crane, as the trailer 333 had a capacity of 130 tons.

Negotiating the narrow streets of Brecon. Stan Williams guiding driver Arthur Matthews.

The Pacific continues forward with assistance from a ballasted Scammell tractor, driven by Archie Morgan with Ron Troath on foot.

The worst now over, the heavy load crosses the bridge and soon leaves Brecon behind.

This view taken at the front of GDW 277 shows (from right) H.P. Wynn, his eldest daughter Judy, her grandfather, Mark Howell, and driver Arthur Matthews.

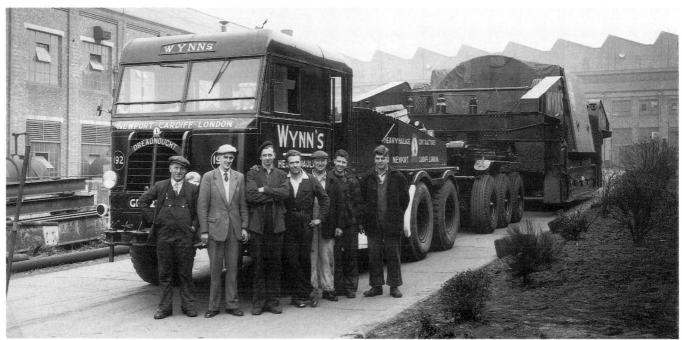

The group in front of GDW 277 (from left) were: Arthur Matthews, the Author, 'Kipper' Kent, Eric Hansen, Bryn Groves (driver), unknown, and Jock Waddington.

A long crane girder on two 16 wheel bogies is manoeuvered around the Old Green Crossing at Newport by Pacific GDW 277 now driven by Rex Evans. The load was en route to Uskmouth Power Station. The Author is shown in front supervising.

Driver Bill Jenkins standing at the front of his Diamond T – GDW 313 (187). A Scammell is on duty at the rear. The load photographed in London, weighed 114 tons.

GDW 313 which entered the fleet in September, 1950 noses her load into position at its destination.

Above: A 98 ton Roll Housing built by Davy-United of Sheffield is transported to Hull Docks for export to Sweden. Diamond T, GDW 800 dating from June, 1951 towing, with veteran Scammell CDW 33 pushing. Shown (from left) is Ron Bailey (driver of the Scammell), Horace Williams and Len Saville.

Left: Fordson Thames 8 ton articulated lorry coupled to Queen Mary trailer carrying a Buckmaster aircraft fuselage. GDW 18 (127) was bought in 1950.

Above: Pacific GDW 585 (196) travelling up Skinner Street, Newport with a transformer en route from Cardiff Docks to Rogerstone Power Station in June, 1957. This Drawbar tractor bore the name 'Helpmate'.

Below: The outfit turns into Westgate Square (of Chartist fame) heading towards Stow Hill.

En route from the English Electric Co. Ltd., Stafford to High Marnham Power Station, this Stator is seen passing through Manchester on 28 wheel trailer No. 666. 'Helpmate' (GDW 585-196) heads the load with 'Dreadnought' (GDW 277-192) behind. Another innovation of H.P. Wynn was the addition of two pairs of 'castor' wheels between the necks, thus increasing her from 24 to 28 wheels.

Above: 196, driven by Bill Pitten, passing along Commercial Street, Newport with a 120 ton transformer en route to Cardiff in the late 1950s.

Opposite top: A 100 ton plus Excavator Base travelling through Coventry on trailer No.555 headed by 'Helpmate'.

Opposite bottom: A 24 wheeled trailer laden with a 120 ton Stator is seen passing over Newport's Town Bridge in the charge of GDW 585 at the front and a Diamond T at the rear, en route to Uskmouth 'A' Power Station.

Above: Accidents do happen. Happily it was not a WYNNS load. This 110 ft long vessel came to rest down a bank on the Skenfrith to Abergavenny road. WYNNS were contracted to recover it and reload it onto the hauliers own equipment.

Opposite top:
The vessel is slowly moved back onto the road by WYNNS Heavy Gang. The tackle wagons are a Bedford 5 tonner FDW 750 (113) dating from January, 1950 and an ex-W.D. Thornycroft.

Opposite bottom:
Back on the road the vessel is ready to be reloaded. The Abergavenny to Ross-on-Wye Road was closed for almost a day whilst the work took place.

Large pieces of masonry being lowered into position from the Town Bridge, Newport, by a WYNNS 25 ton mobile crane.

Trailer No. 666 minus the castors, with a heavy transformer headed by Pacific HDW 122(193) passes through Chipping Norton.

Specially modified necks and bogies of trailer 456 end suspend a 120 ton press from Liverpool Docks to the Midlands. Also of interest is the use of one of the two 'Junior' Pacifics – Valiant' (194) – at the rear.

A heavy transformer en route to the Crumlin Electricity Sub-station travels along the Pontypool to Ystrad Mynach road. The Diamond T leading is EDW 96 (161) whilst at the rear is GDW 313 (187).

The outfit passing Hafodyrynys Colliery, and (below) for the two mile 1 in 7 descent into Crumlin an additional Diamond T has been coupled up at the back to provide extra braking.

Safely at the bottom of Hafodyrynys Hill the outfit is about to negotiate Crumlin Railway Bridge.

An unusual view of the Diamond T negotiating the entrance to Crumlin Sub-station, with H.P. Wynn ensuring the rear end is being manouvered correctly.

Safely through the narrow entrance, the transformer was slid into final position by a WYNNS Heavy Gang. The tackle lorry on the left is a Bedford OWLD 5 ton dropside lorry DDW 173 (130) new in December, 1945.

Scammell 20 ton articulated unit HDW 519 operating with a variety of long loads before the advent of the extending trailer. Carrying Fleet No. 213 she entered service in March, 1953. The driver was always known as 'Barney'

Driver of this Diamond T Drawbar tractor HDW 107 (199) Bill Hayward is seen on the left of this group. Second from the right is Rex Evans driver of the rear tractor, a Scammell – which is not shown. The load, a steel vessel was en route from Babcock and Wilcock Ltd., Oldbury to Liverpool Docks for shipment to Australia. The vessel was 82ft long, 11ft 2ins in diameter, and weighed 71 tons.

Below: HDW 107 driven by Rex Evans coupled to a brand new Scheuerle 150 ton capacity 32 wheel platform trailer leaving Ipswich en route to Newcastle-on-Tyne. Note the use of solid tyres on this occasion to reduce height. But normally she ran on pneumatic tyres.

The independent steering of these bogies is shown to good effect in this view of a turbine arriving at Rogerstone Power Station. The leading tractor is HDW 107. The Author – great grandson of the founder of WYNNS is driving the rear tractor. His father O.G. is seen wearing the cap, whilst his mother is in the light coat.

This unusual combination shows the Diamond T, HDW 107 (199) operating with a special low loader, and carrying a locomotive for The Steel Company of Wales at Margam.
Overleaf: This Electric Locomotive built at Rugby by British Thomson-Houston was conveyed on the same outfit to Liverpool Docks for shipment to Australia.

DANGER
WIDE
LOAD
54
R. WYNN & SONS LTD. NEWPORT.

HDW-107

WYNN'S

This 4 blade propellor with a diameter of 21ft 9ins with square dimensions of 17ft 1ins x 17ft 1ins x 4ft 10ins, and weighing 27 tons was transported in June, 1957 from Manganese Bronze Ltd., Birkenhead to Vickers Armstrongs (Engineers) Ltd., Barrow-in-Furness. It was angled to 30 degrees whilst being negotiated from the loading bay at Birkenhead. For the remainder of the journey it was tilted at 15 degrees. It was for fitting to the new BP Tanker *British Glory* of 21,001 gross tons.

Parked in the Capitol Car Park, Newport, ex-W.D. Scammell 6 x 4 tractor HPP 814 towing a tank transporter trailer laden with a boiler which she had brought from the works of Davey, Paxman & Co. Ltd., at Colchester, Essex.

This Scammell 20 ton articulated lorry HDW 468 (220) dating from February, 1953 was bought from British Road Services at Newport the following year. *On the left* loaded with a ship's propeller in Shaftsbury Street, Newport, and *right* with assembled steelwork on the approach to Caerleon.

Scammell CDW 935 dating from September, 1941 with a boiler loaded on a Carriemore low loader.

Shown at Shaftsbury Street, Newport, outside the Cold Store, another Scammell (225) loaded with a tank locomotive.

A heavy steel fabrication – 23ft long, 16ft wide and 13ft high, en route from Sheppard & Sons, Bridgend, to the Ministry of Works Rocket Research Establishment at Spadeadam in Cumberland.

This series of photographs shows a WYNNS 25 ton mobile crane lifting and installing into position a flood light tower at Alexandra Docks, Newport.

JDW 48 and JDW 49 – two Thornycroft Mighty Antar Drawbar tractors with Crane 100ft trailer. This outfit was built for the Snowy Mountain Hydro-Electric Scheme in Australia and was licensed and tested by WYNNS prior to export. Seen here en route to Uskmouth Power Station in April, 1953, with a 120 ton Stator. This trailer was a sister to WYNNS No. 333 and was bought on our recommendation. The Australians insisted that it was road tested in the United Kingdom before accepting it. The Australian crew accompanied WYNNS personnel who operated the outfit on its test run.

Two wide loads waiting for a Police escort near Sheffield. Both are tank transporter trailers hauled by Diamond T Drawbar tractors – HDW 572 (212) and PDW 321 (266).

Left: A 90 ton transformer about to set out from Uskmouth 'A' Power Station for a Sub-station at Coverack Road, Newport. Diamond T, KDW 560 (184) acquired in December, 1954 heads the load whilst Scammell CDW 33 (87) pushes. On the left is a WYNNS Manchester driver – Wilf Sadler, and driver's mate John Downs is on the right.

Below: Arriving at Coverack Road, Newport, the Scammell is now leading whilst the Diamond T pushes. John Downs is on the trailer (right) whilst Roger Clare stands in front of the tractor unit.

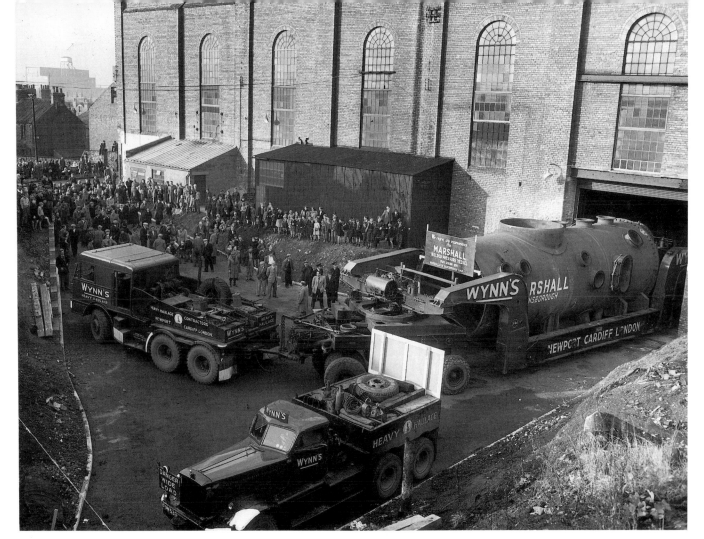

Trailer No. 444 specially widened emerges from the loading bay at Marshalls of Gainsborough. This welded pressure vessel was one of six transported to the National Gas Turbine Establishment, Pyestock, Hampshire.

Scammell KDW 275 (219) dating from September, 1954 pushing a top girder set mounted on two eight wheel bogies, and headed by a Diamond T. These 4 wheel Scammells with ballast box were often used as the second tractor when two were required. 219 was actually an articulated unit when purchased new, being converted at a later date.

AN UNUSUAL JOB

WYNNS Heavy Gang were called on to carry out all manner of difficult tasks, In this series of photographs it shows where they were required to remove a ship's boiler through a hole in the hull and instal a replacement. The vessel was the *Manchester Trader* and was carried out in August, 1958 at the Mountstuart Dry Dock, Cardiff. The whole sequence was carried out under the directions of R.T. & G.P. Wynn, with Ern Adams in charge. This was the first time this had been done.

A. The new boiler – 60 tons, 12ft long with a diameter of 16ft 9ins is lowered into the dry dock where two tank transporter trailers (joined together) with specially constructed timber cradle waits.
B. The new boiler is secured on the cradle.
C. Meanwhile the old boiler is being removed through a hole in the ship's hull.
D. and slowly eased out.
E. Then secured on another pair of trailers with built up cradle.
F. This gives a wider view of the operation.
G. The old boiler has been moved forward out of the way, whilst the new one is brought up adjacent to the hole in the ship's side.
H. The new boiler is slowly moved into position.
I. and enters the hull.
J. The job is nearly completed.

The tractor unit used was a Scammell Drawbar GKC 866 (224). An interesting vehicle built in 1940 by Scammell for Edward Box of Liverpool. She had passed to Pickfords when nationalisation took place in 1948/9. WYNNS acquired her in 1954 with the de-nationalisation of road haulage together with a number of other vehicles. At the same time they also took over the home base of these units, and that was when WYNNS opened their Manchester Depot.

A Reactor Tank of 120 tons carried in top slung position on a 16 wheel trailer en route to the Atomic Station at Dounreay, Caithness-shire. The load is shown negotiating an acute hair-pin bend at Berridale. It was said that the driver of the leading Diamond T, Bryn Groves, signalled to Tommy Cromwell in the pushing Diamond T as they reached the apex of the bend. The author's father O.G. was the only Wynn who had been to the North of Scotland prior to this job, and had told his brother H.P. that the route would be O.K. He was nonetheless relieved when he heard that the outfit had negotiated this particular obstacle. Owing to the necessity of making detours to avoid weak bridges and other obstructions, this journey entailed a total of over 800 miles.

Diamond T, LDW 810 (234) of September, 1955, sporting an experimental Meadows engine, heads this 90 ton paper cylinder. At the delivery point WYNNS Heavy Gang placed this cylinder into final position. Note how wide the trailer frame had to be adjusted to in order to carry this load.

In order to avoid a low bridge at the Newport Town Centre end of Shaftsbury Street, many high loads had to be diverted up Barrack Hill. This photograph shows a 54 R.B. excavator turning into Barrack Hill. The leading vehicle is Diamond T Drawbar tractor NDW 232 (247) driven by Don Hicks.

The excavator travels slowly up Barrack Hill with the help of two Diamond T's pushing – EDW 95 and PDW 927.

Nearing the top of Barrack Hill – a 1 in 6 incline – the excavator and attendant Diamond T tractors emerge above the clouds.

WYNNS operated a large fleet of tar tankers. In this view five tank trailers are seen connected to Scammell articulated tractor units (from the left): HDW 468 (220), GGU 262 (255), LDW 227 (227), GXC 463 (256) and HDW 469 (221). Fleet Nos. 255 and 256 dated from 1941 and were new to the War-time Petrol Pool who had sold them to Shell-Mex after hostilities. WYNNS acquired them in 1957. 220 and 221 were new to British Road Services Newport Branch in February, 1953, and were bought on de-nationalisation the following year, whilst 227 came new in May, 1955 straight from Scammell. Besides tar Wynns also carried chemicals and acids.

A pair of Guy Warrior Light 8 eight wheeled tar tankers UDW 875 (153) and WDW 63 (159) which joined the WYNNS fleet in 1960.

Part of the large fleet of tipping vehicles and earth-moving equipment operated by WYNNS. This photograph from the early 1960s shows Guy, Austin and Thames Trader tippers together with Drott machine being used in land reclamation. Whilst many of the tipper fleet were based at the Cardiff Depot, WYNNS were important members of the Monmouthshire Tipper Association.

A selection of Guy lorries – tippers, flats and artics – belonging to WYNNS.

Above: Electrical equipment loaded on WYNNS lightweight articulated low loaders – LDW 835 (235) Bedford 'S' type from October 1955, YDW 351 (143) Guy from 1961, ODW 479 (259) Commer of 1957 and YDW 421 (136) dating from 1961. This latter vehicle was coupled to a specially converted trailer to carry equipment in slung position – the conversion having been carried out at WYNNS Newport Headquarters.

Left: Guy artic PDW 412 (267) dating from 1958 coupled to a Queen Mary trailer loaded with steelwork from Messrs. Stewart & Lloyds, Newport.

Right: A piece of fabricated metalwork being hauled on a Bedford 'S' type articulated low loader ODW 480 (260) which was new in 1957.

A

B

On 3rd April, 1954, WYNNS held the first of what was to become an Annual Dinner, at the Tudor Rooms, Risca Road, Newport. In subsequent years the scope of the event was extended to include a Dance and the showing of films devoted to the work of the firm over the previous year. These were held in Newport's premier hotels.

In this series of photographs, members of the family, staff and employees are shown together with invited guests.

A. *(from left):* Sam Wynn, Norman E. Lamb (who responded on behalf of the guests), O.G. Wynn, E.E. Cashmore (who also responded for the guests). Percy Clarke and Cyril Bates.

B. Reg Blake, H.P. Wynn, Humphrey Williams (WYNNS second Engineer), the Author, Tony Knight, Arthur Matthews, Fred 'Bomber' Smith, Harry 'Oscar' Thomas, Bill Barrell, Albert Brown and Jack James.

C. Bill Hayward, Roy Pobjoy, Ted Ellaway, Lloyd Jones, Jack Perrott, Fred Manley (Yard Foreman), Gordon Pearce, Harry Fowles, Bob Wynn, Bernie Hodge (Welshpool Manager), G.P. (Gordon) Wynn, and Bert Woods (Cardiff Manager).

D. *(clockwise from right):* Lloyd Jones, Bill Hayward, Dai Squires, Dan Davies, Ted Morris, Ern Cooling, Alan Brown (Heavy Gang) who had completed 50 years service, E.E. Cashmore, Percy Clarke, Cyril Bates, J.D.R. Jones, Bill Jones, Eric Scott, Roy Pobjoy and Ted Ellaway.

E. (clockwise from left): Ern Adams, Noel Wynn, Dawson Burns, Harry Charrington, a Guest, Edmund Walker, R.T. Wynn, Bill Bennett (Timber Haulier) who had completed 50 years service, Bill Twycross (Watchman), Ralph Toombs, Tom White and Jimmy Cliss.

F. O.G. Wynn (the Author's father) proposing the toast to the guests.

G. R.T. Wynn responding to the toast to the Company. On his left is the Mayor of Newport, Councillor William Pinnell, BEM.

H. Alan Brown, one of three employees presented with a television set to mark 50 years service. His three sons – Gordon, Dick and Len also worked for WYNNS, together with Gordon's two sons, Robert and Leslie. The others receiving awards for 50 years service were Jim Edwards (Carpenter) and Bill Bennett. Twelve employees who had completed between 26 and 38 years service were presented with a clock or gold watch.

D

F

H

Some idea of the difficulty experienced in moving a heavy load in a congested town centre is shown in these three photographs.

Opposite left: A Diamond T, NDW 232 proceeds along High Street, Newport. Driver's Mate 'Ginger' Barry and the Author assist with directions to the driver. A Scammell is coupled to the rear of the outfit.

Opposite bottom: The excavator enters the Westgate Square and then into Commercial Street.

Above: Continuing along Commercial Street, past the junction with Corn Street – the load has only travelled 200 yards since the first photograph was taken – and there was a long way to go yet.

With the advent of open-cast coal mining from the late 1940s WYNNS were increasingly involved with the movement of a vast number of excavators, primarily 54 RBs, 1201 and 802 Limas. Such was the volume of this work that it became the norm for outfits to be worked for four weeks at a stretch. The crews only coming home for one weekend in four – leaving the kit, they travelled home by train on the Friday night, returning on the Monday morning. The main areas served with this work were the Midlands, South Wales, The Peak District, The Pennines, and The Moors.

An aerial view showing the Shaftsbury Street, Newport, yard of Robert Wynn & Sons Ltd (centre). In the foreground is the railway bridge over the River Usk carrying the South Wales to London (Paddington) main line, and bottom right the present Town Bridge under construction.

In the early 1960s WYNNS had outgrown the Shaftsbury Street premises, and whilst the offices remained there for a while, a comprehensive workshop and storage facility was built at Albany Street, Newport.

The two views above of the Albany Street facility, show (left) a Guy 8 wheel rigid tar tanker YDW 115 (156) receiving attention whilst a Thames Trader 4 wheel tipper XWO 218 (71) moves forward over an inspection pit, and (right) in the foreground a pair of sixteen wheel bogies are being steam cleaned.

Another view of the workshops at Albany Street, Newport.

The Cardiff Depot of Robert Wynn & Sons Ltd at Collingdon Road, West Dock.

A 24 ton gross Guy Invincible 8 wheeler TDW 991 (294) dating from 1960 carrying a ship's propeller is shown on Cardiff Road, Newport, by Belle Vue Park.

Guy Invincible articulated unit PDW 600 couple to a semi-trailer laden with steelwork. With Fleet No. 269 this vehicle was bought new in 1958 and coincided with WYNNS becoming agent for Guy Motors in South Wales. The agency was held by the WYNNS subsidiary company – Crindau Garages Ltd.

WYNNS became involved with the transport of steel-protected tubes, used for imported methane gas. This photograph shows part of the fleet of 40ft. artics employed on this work at Stewart & Lloyd's works, Corporation Road, Newport.

Left: This 20ft diameter forged ring is mounted on a tilting table to keep the width of the load to a minimum. The drawing vehicle is Guy Invincible 6 wheeler WDW 100 (100), which is shown on arrival at Uskside Engineering Works, Newport, after its journey from Darlington Forge, Middlesbrough.

Below left: A rare bonneted Guy Invincible 6x4 articulated tractor unit – YDW 521 (101) loaded with an excavator. Shown at the Malpas Dual Carriageway, Newport, waiting for a Police escort.

Below: YDW 521 seen at WYNNS Shaftsbury Street yard laden with a Saddle tank locomotive. Note the new Scheuerle 8 wheel steering bogie.

Above: In the period 1960/61 WYNNS added four Scammell Highwayman articulated units to the fleet for general service. VDW 324 (180) is seen with a D8 Bulldozer.
Below: VDW 325 (181) is shown outside Malpas Barracks, Newport with a wide stainless steel fermenting vessel which had been transported from Leeds.

Above: Two Scammell low loaders carrying Euclid dump trucks. The leading vehicle is YDW 522 (178).
Below: WDW 383 (179) shown negotiating a tight exit from the works at Leeds with another Fermenting Vessel.

Above: Moving a ship's boiler at Vickers in Barrow-in-Furness on a 24 wheel trailer (No. 666) with a Pacific tractor at the front and a Diamond T at the back. The boiler was destined to be installed in the B.P. Tanker Company's 21,001 gross ton tanker *British Faith* which was completed in 1958. Note castor wheels between the necks in retracted position.

Opposite top: Moving the starboard aft boiler for P & O's liner *Oriana* at Barrow-in-Furness on trailer (No. 555). Note the man on top of the load armed with a wooden pole with which to lift low lying telephone wires.

Opposite bottom: P & O's 41,915 gross ton passenger liner *Oriana* was completed by Vickers at Barrow-in-Furness in 1960. In this view WYNNS were transporting her port forward boiler, again on trailer 555. Robert Wynn & Sons Ltd were called on to move much heavy material for this and other shipbuilders, and on many occasions only had to provide transport for quite short distances within the area of the shipyard.

WYNNS were approached by Richard Thomas & Baldwin Ltd to move a 146 ton Excavator in one piece to new workings at their Limestone Quarry at Trefil, near Tredegar in the shortest possible time. The task was accomplished during one weekend.

Above: This photograph shows the load ascending a 1 in 6 gradient. Five tractors were used to haul the load up the incline – A Ward La France wrecker EDW 599 (203) driven by Bryn Lavender is coupled to Foden 112 which in turn is on the front of Pacific 192. At the rear is Pacific 196 pushed by Scammell lightweight 210. The trailer is the 24 wheel 200 ton capacity '444' evolved from the original 16 wheel 130 ton capacity '333'.

Below: The excavator about to negotiate a severe left hand bend with a steep incline. Note the excavator is in one piece, and the ruggedness of the Welsh hillside at Trefil. H.P. Wynn records the move on his cine camera.

Above: On easier ground the excavator still needed three tractor units.

Right: The excavator being unloaded at new workings.

109

The Spencer Steelworks of Richard Thomas & Baldwin Ltd was the largest in Europe. During its construction between 1959 and 1962 WYNNS carried more than 10,000 tons of plant and equipment from Newport Docks alone to the Llanwern site under contract. Loads included gantry girders and heavy electrical equipment – the heaviest being 110 ton castings. The photographs (*opposite*) show castings being loaded onto a WYNNS outfit from the Bristol City Line's vessel *New York City* at Newport Docks, and (*above*) about to be unloaded on site. Many thousands of tons of shale were carried to the site by free-lance contractors, and WYNNS maintained a 24 hour salvage service for recovering those that fell by the wayside.

Above: WYNNS owned two heavy mobile gantries each of 75 tons capacity which were used at Llanwern. These had originally been built by the Germans for use in the Channel Islands on submarines in the Second World War. Post-war they had been bought by the Steel Company of Wales to assist in the construction of their Margam works, and on completion R.T. Wynn had quickly bought them. They were a valuable asset to the firm, and were widely used.

An unusual sight by any standards – five tractors being used to haul a 185 ton casting en route from the works of Davy-United, Sheffield to Northern Aluminium at Rogerstone, Monmouthshire. The load is being carried on a 32 wheeled trailer – which consisted of the frame of '666' but with the addition of two brand new 16 wheel bogies which later became '456' once the new assembly was delivered by Cranes of Dereham. The load is headed by a Pacific and double-headed by a Diamond T, with three more Diamond Ts pushing at the rear. The photograph was taken as the outfit moved on easier ground near Buckingham. When the load reached Gloucester it was transhipped onto a railway truck to avoid the weak bridge at Over and then reloaded within 1/2 mile back onto the WYNNS trailer.

WYNNS

Above: This 23ft. diameter ship's propellor is tilted to an angle of 30 degrees to enable it to pass through this gap of 16ft 2ins at Black Barrow. The motive power is provided by Diamond T, LDW 810 (234).

Below: '666' loaded with a 140 ton English Electric Transformer from Stafford is headed by Pacific HDW 122 (193) with Diamond T, RDW 976 (281) at the back.

Above: After a Bath & West Show Gill French with Diamond T, TDW 241 (279) delivered this lifeboat to Balshoms Shipyard at Poole.

Below: Used by WYNNS for over 20 years these Diamond T drawbar tractors were continuously rebuilt and modified in their own workshops. Note the modern cab fitted to LDW 810, whilst the tractor at the rear has the old style cab.

Left: Two views of Diamond T, EDW 96 double-heading the Pacific GDW 585 driven by Bill Pitten on the start of the long climb up the 1 in 6 Barrack Hill, Newport. The load is a 140 ton transformer en route to Uskmouth 'A' Power Station. The load is given extra help by two more Diamond T's pushing at the rear. The Author has his back to the camera.

Above: Again heading up Barrack Hill in the early 1960s – a turbine casing hauled by three Diamond T tractors, two at the front and one (out of sight) behind. The load en route to Rogerstone Power Station, has Jack Stanton coupled to the load with the author driving the front tractor – NDW 232. Bill Hayward is shown walking backwards, with Stan Anderson, the new Chief Engineer on the left.

Two impressive views of WYNNS in action:
Above: Two Pacifics and a Diamond T transporting a heavy transformer, and
Below: Pacific GDW 277 passing Rugby School with a Meaford 160 ton Stator from B.T.H.

New to the WYNNS fleet in 1963 was this 48 wheel trailer capable of carrying 300 tons. No. 789. The group in front is *(from left)* Arthur Matthews, H.P. Wynn, Eddie Clark, Stan Williams, Roddy Campbell, Tommy Cromwell.

As so often with new equipment, problems can occur. Trailer 789 whilst carrying its first load had hydraulic ram trouble on the Leeds Ring Road. Three days were lost whilst repairs were effected. Seen nearest the camera is Stan Williams, Arthur Matthews with cigarette, and H.P. Wynn in the trilby, looking less than happy.

Trailer No. 789 carrying another English Electric Transformer. The load is hauled by three Pacifics. Driver Tommy Cromwell is on the front with Bryn Groves and Bill Pitten pushing.

A considerable number of tanks were transported from Army bases around the country. The one illustrated was a Bridge Laying tank en route from Ludgershall to John Cashmore's at Newport for breaking up.

The only time that the 'Festival of Britain' girders were used on another job – this 105 ton gun mounting was moved from Woolwich Arsenal to Shoeburyness, Essex. Shown with the load are *(from left):* Don Hicks, 'Kipper' Kent, H.P. Wynn, the Author and two Police Officers, the escort.

A 24 wheel trailer leaving the works of Metropolitan Vickers at Trafford Park, Manchester with a 130 ton transformer. Note the 'V'-bar fitted to the front of the Diamond T. This WYNNS innovation freed the drivers hands from steering the tractor thus enabling him to give maximum power.

Epitomising the post-war WYNNS fleet. This 1963 registered Cummins-engined Diamond T 3630 DW driven by Maurice White heads this excavator as it passes through Pontypool Town Centre. Another Diamond T is pushing at the back. The Author is standing infront. The Publisher of this book, Paul Heaton, who was a Police Motor Cyclist at the time was escorting the load, and when this photograph was taken, already had the traffic stopped at the Clarence.

WYNNS

WYNNS

100 YEARS

Robert Wynn & Sons Limited

Head Office: 50, Shaftsbury Street, Newport, Mon.
Cardiff: Collingdon Road, West Dock.
London: 752, Arch, Enid Street, SE16.
Manchester: Robert Wynn & Sons (Manchester) Ltd., Broadfield Road, Moss Side, 14.

To mark their Centenary in 1963 Robert Wynn and Sons Ltd held a parade through the streets of Newport, showing the various developments which had taken place in the firm's history.
Above: From the horse and cart.

Opposite top: R.T. Wynn is shown saluting the John Fowler steam road locomotive DW 2121 from 1920 which is drawing the 1890 built boiler wagon.

Opposite bottom: Solid rubber tyred low loader trailer. In the background can be seen Newport Castle.

20 TON CAPACITY STEAM TRACTOR
& (AS USED IN 1927)
SOLID RUBBER TYRE TR
(AS USED IN

WYNN'S 371

Enthusiastic Crowds looking on as a Guy with a Queen Mary trailer passes by.

A scene spanning four of WYNNS main areas of operation: tankers, mobile cranes, round timber extraction, and light heavy haulage.

300 ton capacity, 48 wheel trailer No. 789 passing (above) the Old Green Crossing, and *(below)* The Westgate Square, Newport, with H.P. Wynn looking on. This trailer needed expertise to operate when empty, let alone when loaded.

Pictured in front of the John Fowler Steam Road Locomotive DW 2121 celebrating the Centenary of Robert Wynn and Sons are (from left): H.P. (Percy) Wynn, R.T. Wynn, O.G. (George) Wynn, G.P. (Gordon) Wynn, and Noel Wynn. The Author John took the photograph. Sam had died in 1962.

Author's Note: I hope that you have enjoyed this book on the first hundred years of Robert Wynn and Sons Ltd. In my next book I hope to bring the story up to date, however, I am always endeavouring to obtain additional material on the firm, for example we were actively concerned with the development of the 'Concorde', taking many wing and fuselage sections from Filton to Weybridge, but unfortunately I have no photographs. I would be interested in hearing from anyone who can assist.

Please contact me at
7, Quebec Close,
Glasllwch,
Newport,
Gwent, NP9 3RA.
Tel. 01633-251388.